# BARR-C:2018

Embedded C Coding Standard

# Embedded C Coding Standard

by Michael Barr

**BARR group**

The Embedded Systems Experts

**Edition: BARR-C:2018 | barrgroup.com**

**Embedded C Coding Standard**

by Michael Barr

Copyright © 2018 Integrated Embedded, LLC (dba Barr Group). All rights reserved.

Published by:

> Barr Group
> 20251 Century Blvd, Suite 330
> Germantown, MD 20874

This book may be purchased in print and electronic editions. A free online edition is also available. For more information see https://barrgroup.com/coding-standard.

While every precaution has been taken in the preparation of this book, the publisher and author assume no responsibility for errors or omissions, or for damages resulting from the use of the information contained herein. Compliance with the coding standard rules in this book neither ensures against software defects nor legal liability. Product safety and security are your responsibility.

Barr Group, the Barr Group logo, The Embedded Systems Experts, and BARR-C are trademarks or registered trademarks of Integrated Embedded, LLC. Any other trademarks used in this book are property of their respective owners.

ISBN-13: 978-1-72112-798-6
ISBN-10: 1-72112-798-4

# Document License

By obtaining Barr Group's copyrighted "Embedded C Coding Standard" (the "Document"), you are agreeing to be bound by the terms of this Document License ("Agreement").

1. RIGHTS GRANTED. For good and valuable consideration, the receipt, adequacy, and sufficiency of which is hereby acknowledged, Barr Group grants you a license to use the Document as follows: You may publish the Document for your own internal use and for the use of your internal staff in conducting your business only. By obtaining a copy of the Document, you expressly agree to the terms of this Agreement.

2. RIGHTS RESERVED. Except as expressly permitted herein, no rights in or to the Document are granted to you. Barr Group (on behalf of itself and its Affiliates) retains all other rights in and to the Document, anywhere in the world. Specifically, you acknowledge and agree: (i) that Barr Group holds the copyright for the Document; (ii) that the Document and any works derived therefrom may not be published or shared except as permitted in Section 1 above; (iii) that you shall take appropriate measures regarding limitations on publishing and sharing, including the incorporation of appropriate copyright markings and notations on limitations of publishing and sharing, as described in this Agreement. If you fail to include these required copyright markings and notations, you agree that such copies are unauthorized copies of the copyright material and that these unauthorized copies infringe Barr Group's copyright of the Document. If you prepare any new works, translations or derivative works from the Document, you hereby agree that your rights for these new works, translations, or derivative works are limited to your private (e.g., company internal) use.

3. DISCLAIMERS AND LIMITATION ON LIABILITY. You agree to hold harmless, defend, and indemnify Barr Group, its owners and officers, employees, and subcontractors, to the full extent permitted by law, for any claims brought in relation to, or use of, the Document. You bear full responsibility for determining whether the contents of the Document and its derivations are safe and appropriate for the purposes of your uses. In addition: (a) THE DOCUMENT IS PROVIDED "AS IS" WITHOUT REPRESENTATION OR WARRANTY OF ANY KIND. TO THE MAXIMUM EXTENT PERMITTED BY APPLICABLE LAW, BARR GROUP EXPRESSLY DISCLAIMS ANY AND ALL WARRANTIES, STATUTORY, EXPRESSED OR IMPLIED, INCLUDING, BUT NOT LIMITED, TO ANY IMPLIED WARRANTIES OF MERCHANTABILITY, FITNESS FOR A PARTICULAR PURPOSE, AND NON-INFRINGEMENT WITH REGARD TO THE DOCUMENT. (b) In no event shall Barr Group be liable for any damages whatsoever (including, but not limited to, special, incidental, consequential, or indirect damages for personal injury, any and all other third party claims, loss of business profits, business interruption, loss of business information, or any other pecuniary loss, attorneys' fees and litigation costs) resulting from or related to this Agreement or the use of the Document (whether or not Barr Group knew or should have known of the possibility of any such damages) or any third party claim that the Document as delivered to you hereunder, infringes any copyright or trademark right or misappropriates any trade secret of any third party.

4. GOVERNING LAW; JURISDICTION; VENUE. This Agreement shall be construed in accordance with the laws of the State of Maryland without giving effect to its conflicts of laws rules. Any dispute arising out of, connected with or relating to this Agreement, shall be brought in either the state court of general jurisdiction in Montgomery County or the U.S. District Court for the District of Maryland, which the parties agree shall be the venue and exclusive forum in which to adjudicate any case or controversy arising from or relating to this Agreement. Each party irrevocably submits to the jurisdiction of such courts and waives any objections to either the jurisdiction of or venue in such courts. In the event Barr Group prevails in any dispute arising out of, connected with, or relating to this Agreement, you shall pay Barr Group any and all costs associated with such dispute, including, without limitation, reasonable attorneys' fees.

5. SEVERABILITY; CONSIDERATION. Every part of this Agreement shall be considered severable. If for any reason any party of this Agreement is held to be invalid, that determination shall not impair or otherwise affect the enforceability of the other parts of this Agreement. By obtaining the Document, you acknowledge and agree that the consideration underlying this Agreement is the mutual promises and covenants herein and your use of, and access to, the Document subject to the terms and conditions of this Agreement.

# Contents

Introduction ............................................................................................................... 1

    Purpose of the Standard ........................................................................................ 1

    Guiding Principles ................................................................................................. 2

    MISRA C .................................................................................................................. 4

    C++ vs. C .................................................................................................................. 5

    Enforcement Guidelines ........................................................................................ 5

    Deviation Procedure .............................................................................................. 6

    Customization ......................................................................................................... 7

    Acknowledgements ................................................................................................ 7

1    General Rules ...................................................................................................... 8

    1.1    Which C? ...................................................................................................... 8

    1.2    Line Widths ................................................................................................. 9

    1.3    Braces ......................................................................................................... 10

    1.4    Parentheses ................................................................................................ 11

    1.5    Common Abbreviations ........................................................................... 12

    1.6    Casts ............................................................................................................ 13

    1.7    Keywords to Avoid .................................................................................. 14

    1.8    Keywords to Frequent ............................................................................. 15

2    Comment Rules ................................................................................................ 17

    2.1    Acceptable Formats .................................................................................. 17

    2.2    Locations and Content ............................................................................. 18

# 3 White Space Rules ........................................................................................... 21
## 3.1 Spaces ............................................................................................... 21
## 3.2 Alignment ......................................................................................... 23
## 3.3 Blank Lines ....................................................................................... 24
## 3.4 Indentation ....................................................................................... 25
## 3.5 Tabs .................................................................................................. 27
## 3.6 Non-Printing Characters ................................................................. 28

# 4 Module Rules ................................................................................................. 29
## 4.1 Naming Conventions ...................................................................... 29
## 4.2 Header Files ..................................................................................... 30
## 4.3 Source Files ...................................................................................... 31
## 4.4 File Templates .................................................................................. 32

# 5 Data Type Rules ............................................................................................. 33
## 5.1 Naming Conventions ...................................................................... 33
## 5.2 Fixed-Width Integers ...................................................................... 34
## 5.3 Signed and Unsigned Integers ....................................................... 35
## 5.4 Floating Point .................................................................................. 36
## 5.5 Structures and Unions .................................................................... 37
## 5.6 Booleans ........................................................................................... 39

# 6 Procedure Rules ............................................................................................. 40
## 6.1 Naming Conventions ...................................................................... 40
## 6.2 Functions .......................................................................................... 42
## 6.3 Function-Like Macros ..................................................................... 44
## 6.4 Threads of Execution ...................................................................... 45
## 6.5 Interrupt Service Routines ............................................................. 46

| | | |
|---|---|---|
| 7 | Variable Rules | 48 |
| | 7.1 Naming Conventions | 48 |
| | 7.2 Initialization | 50 |
| 8 | Statement Rules | 51 |
| | 8.1 Variable Declarations | 51 |
| | 8.2 Conditional Statements | 52 |
| | 8.3 Switch Statements | 53 |
| | 8.4 Loops | 54 |
| | 8.5 Jumps | 55 |
| | 8.6 Equivalence Tests | 56 |
| Appendix A: Table of Abbreviations | | 57 |
| Appendix B: Header File Template | | 59 |
| Appendix C: Source File Template | | 60 |
| Appendix D: Example Program | | 61 |
| Bibliography | | 69 |
| Index | | 70 |

# Introduction

## *Purpose of the Standard*

Barr Group's *Embedded C Coding Standard* was designed specifically to reduce the number of programming defects in embedded software. By following this coding standard, firmware developers not only reduce hazards to users and time spent in the debugging stage of their projects but also improve the maintainability and portability of their software. Together these outcomes can greatly lower the cost of developing high-reliability embedded software.

This "BARR-C" coding standard is different from other coding standards. Rather than being based on the stylistic preferences of the authors, the rules in this standard were selected for their ability to minimize defects. When it was the case that one rule had the ability to prevent more defects from being made by programmers than an alternative rule for a similar aspect of coding, that more impactful rule was chosen. For example, the stylistic rules for when and where to place curly braces were selected on the basis of their ability to reduce bugs across a whole program.

Individual rules that are objectively expected to reduce the number of defects in this way are tagged with the following "Keeps Bugs Out" icon:

Clearly, no set of coding rules will be able to eliminate 100% of the defects from embedded systems. Interactions between electronics and software as well as between inter-connected systems are complex by their nature. Even if there existed a team of programmers able to code perfectly and they followed all possible defect-minimizing rules, defects in the product could still occur as a result of: mistakes in the project requirements; misunderstandings of the requirements by implementers; oversights in the architecture of the system and/or software; insufficient handling of hardware failures or other exceptional run-time circumstances; etc.

Other important reasons to adopt this coding standard include increased readability and portability of source code. The result of which is reduced cost of code maintenance and reuse. Adopting the complete set of rules in this coding standard (i.e., not just the defect reducers) benefits a team of developers and its larger organization by helping to reduce the time required by individuals to understand the work of their peers and predecessors.

We recommend that the BARR-C coding standard be applied to your project as part of a broader effort to improve your organization's embedded software development and quality assurance processes. Relative to the risks to human users of your projects, of course, an appropriate software development process may be lightweight but must emphasize the importance of system and software architecture to prevent and recover from run-time hazards as well as professional training for all programmers in this and other aspects of their work.[1] At a minimum, your process should include not only a coding standard but also at least the use of version control and defect tracking tools, formal architecture/design reviews and peer code reviews, as well as automated source code scans via one or more static analysis tools.

## *Guiding Principles*

To focus our attention and eliminate internal conflict over items that are too-often viewed by programmers as personal stylistic preferences, this coding standard was developed in accordance with the following guiding principles:

1. Individual programmers do not own the software they write. All software development is work for hire for an employer or a client and, thus, the end product should be constructed in a workmanlike manner.

2. It is cheaper and easier to prevent a bug from creeping into code than it is to find and kill it after it has entered. A key strategy in this fight is to write code in which the compiler, linker, or a static analysis tool can detect such defects automatically—i.e., before the code is allowed to execute.

---

[1] Whenever humans could be injured or killed by a product malfunction or insecurity, appropriate safety guidelines should be followed. This book is NOT a safety standard.

3. For better or worse (well, mostly worse), the ISO C Programming Language "Standard" permits a considerable amount of variation between compilers.[2] The ISO C Standard's "implementation-defined," "unspecified," and "undefined" behaviors, along with "locale-specific options", mean that even programs compiled from identical source code but via different "ISO C"-compliant compilers may behave very differently at run-time. Such gray areas in the C language standard greatly reduce the portability of source code that is not carefully crafted.

4. The reliability, readability, efficiency, and sometimes portability of source code is more important than programmer convenience..

5. There are many sources of defects in software programs. The original team of programmers will create some defects. Programmers who later maintain, extend, port, and/or reuse the resulting source code may create additional defects—including as a result of misunderstandings of the original code.

    - The number and severity of defects introduced by the original programmer(s) can be reduced through disciplined conformance with certain coding practices, such as the placement of constants to the left side of an equivalence (==) test.

    - The number and severity of defects introduced by maintenance programmers can also be reduced by the original programmer. For example, appropriate use of portable fixed-width integer types (e.g., `int32_t`) ensures that no future port of the code will encounter an unexpected overflow.

    - The number and severity of defects introduced by maintenance programmers can also be reduced through the disciplined use of consistent commenting and stylistic practices, so that everyone in an organization can more easily understand the meaning and proper use of variables, functions, and modules.

---

[2] See, e.g., [C90] and [C99].

6. To be effective, coding standards must be enforceable. Thus, when it is the case that two or more alternative rules would equally prevent defects, the more easily enforced rule is the better choice.

In the absence of a needed rule herein or a conflict within the coding standard your team commits to follow, the spirit of the above principles should be applied to guide the decision.

## MISRA C

The *MISRA C:2012 – Guidelines for the Use of the C Language in Critical Systems* (see [MISRA-C]) defines a subset of the C programming language that is safer—albeit also more restrictive—than the rules in this BARR-C coding standard.

If you are designing products that could kill or injure one or more people, the MISRA C guidelines are important to study and should be made part of your project's coding standard. The MISRA C guidelines are now in their third edition and have been practiced for over two decades. Chances are that the authors of the MISRA C are more knowledgeable than you of the risks of using C in safety-critical systems.

In the present edition, every effort has been made to ensure that BARR-C's rules can be combined with some or all of MISRA-C:2012's guidelines. Specifically:

- To the extent that a collection of the rules herein define a subset of the C programming language (e.g., limitations on the use of the `register` and `goto` keywords), they are never more restrictive than the MISRA C guidelines. Put another way, MISRA-C:2012 defines a subset of the C language that is itself a subset of the BARR-C rules.
- To the extent that a collection of the rules herein place stylistic limitations on programmers (e.g., restricting the format of function or variable names), these never contradict the MISRA C guidelines. In other words, BARR-C comprises a C style guide that is complementary to MISRA C, which does not make any recommendations related purely to style.

A 2018 survey found that together these standards were the primary basis of the project-specific coding standards followed by more than 40% of firmware designers.

## C++ vs. C

Though the title of this book only explicitly includes the C language, embedded programmers working in C++ (or a mix of the two languages) are also able to reduce the number of defects in their programs by following the rules herein. This is because the syntax of C++ follows closely from C and many lines of C++ source code rely only on C syntax.

It is important to note, however, that C++ is a substantially larger and more complex language than C and contains a number of features that have no equivalent in C. If you are following the BARR-C rules in C++ you should strongly consider adopting other coding standard rules, perhaps choosing from those suggested by [MISRA-C++], [Sutter], and/or [Holub].

As embedded software developers, our focus remains primarily on C, which is the primary programming language for about 70% of professional firmware designers. A longitudinal review of industry surveys spanning 2005 to 2018 shows that C was not only reliably the most widely-used language but that it actually increased its market share from 50% to about 70% in those years. Within the embedded systems community, it appears the peak year for C++ was 2006.

## Enforcement Guidelines

Conformance with all of the rules in this coding standard is deemed mandatory. Non-conforming code should preferably be detected: primarily via automated scans (i.e., static analysis); secondarily via peer code reviews; or, in the absence of those options, informal discovery. Upon detection, any non-conforming code should be made to meet all of the rules herein.

There are commercial static analysis tools that can be used to automatically check for non-compliance with many of the rules of this and other coding standards. Tools pre-configured to detect violations of the enforceable subset of rules in this coding standard are requested to refer to it as the "BARR-C:2018" standard.

When changing to a new coding standard, decisions must be made regarding legacy code. Few development teams have time to revisit the style of pre-existing source code libraries.

With respect to legacy code we suggest that:

- It is generally best to leave working legacy code alone. Unless, of course, life and limb are on the line.
- Any decision to bring legacy source code into conformance with the rules herein should be made for one module (i.e., .h header file and .c source file) or library at a time. The best time to make such stylistic changes is often when the module or library also requires functional changes.

Note that changes relating to the use and/or placement of white space (e.g., replacement of tabs with spaces) should be made in a version control check-in that is distinct from functional changes to the same code. This is to ensure the maximal utility of the source code differencing features of version control tools with respect to functional changes made before and after the white space changes.

## *Deviation Procedure*

All source code that is submitted for a product release shall conform to all of the rules herein, except if its specific deviations have been documented and approved.

At the project level, rules that indicate a specific quantity of something (e.g., the number of characters per indent or maximum lines in a function) can be changed to enforce a different quantity that works better in the actual development tools. The specific quantity is not typically the key property of these types of rules.

At the level of source code modules, it is only acceptable to deviate from this coding standard with the approval of the project manager. The approver's name and the reasoning supporting the deviation shall be documented as closely as possible to the actual deviation(s). For example, a single deviation in a single function should be documented in a comment above or within the implementation code—whichever will be clearest to the next reader. By contrast, a module-wide deviation may be better documented in the comments at the top of the source file.

## *Customization*

This document as well as the selection and arrangement of the rules it comprises is Copyright © 2018 by Barr Group. It is permissible for individual project teams, whole companies, and others to adopt all or a subset of the rules herein as their coding standard. Indeed, we are happy that many readers of earlier editions have done this and hope that many more will. Adoption of the rules as presented herein may be done simply by identifying *"Barr Group's Embedded C Coding Standard"* (alternatively, "BARR-C:2018") as the source of your rules.

To help development teams customize this coding standard to meet their project- or company-specific needs, an editable version of this document is available for license and download at barrgroup.com/coding-standard.

Your full legal obligations in relation to the use of this copyrighted work are described at the front of this book.

## *Acknowledgements*

Though my name is listed as author, the development and maintenance of this *Embedded C Coding Standard* book has been a collaborative effort that began more than a decade ago and involved most of the people currently at Barr Group as well as many other members of the embedded software community. I am specifically grateful to Salomon Singer and Joe Perret for helping me make the 2008 edition of the book a reality; to Gary Stringham for working closely with me on the more technical updates in this 2018 edition; and to all of the multitude who commented on specific rules or proposed changes, reviewed drafts of any edition, or provided other types of feedback across the years.

# 1 General Rules

## 1.1 Which C?

**Rules**:

a. All programs shall be written to comply with the C99 version of the ISO C Programming Language Standard.[3]

b. Whenever a C++ compiler is used, appropriate compiler options shall be set to restrict the language to the selected version of ISO C.

c. The use of proprietary compiler language keyword extensions, `#pragma`, and inline assembly shall be kept to the minimum necessary to get the job done and be localized to a small number of device driver modules that interface directly to hardware.

d. Preprocessor directive `#define` shall not be used to alter or rename any keyword or other aspect of the programming language.

**Example**:

```
#define begin   {        // Don't do something like this...
#define end     }        // ... nor this.
...
    for (int row = 0; row < MAX_ROWS; row++)
    begin
        ...
    end                  // Let C be C, not some language you once loved.
```

**Reasoning**: To clearly define the rules in the rest of this standard, it is important that we first agree on the baseline programming language specification.

**Enforcement**: These rules shall be enforced via compiler setup and code reviews.

---

[3] C99-compatible compilers offer many valuable improvements over older compilers, such as C++-style comments, Boolean and fixed-width integer types, inline functions, and local variable declarations anywhere within a function body.

## *1.2 Line Widths*

**Rules**:

   a. The width of all lines in a program shall be limited to a maximum of 80 characters.

**Reasoning**: From time-to-time, peer reviews and other code examinations are conducted on printed pages. To be useful, such print-outs must be free of distracting line wraps as well as missing (i.e., past the right margin) characters. Line width rules also ease on-screen side-by-side code differencing.

**Enforcement**: Violations of this rule shall be detected by an automated scan during each build.

# Embedded C Coding Standard

## 1.3 Braces

**Rules**:

a. Braces shall always surround the blocks of code (a.k.a., compound statements), following `if`, `else`, `switch`, `while`, do, and `for` statements; single statements and empty statements following these keywords shall also always be surrounded by braces.

b. Each left brace (`{`) shall appear by itself on the line below the start of the block it opens. The corresponding right brace (`}`) shall appear by itself in the same position the appropriate number of lines later in the file.

**Example**:

```
{
    if (depth_in_ft > 10) dive_stage = DIVE_DEEP;      // This is legal...
    else if (depth_in_ft > 0)
        dive_stage = DIVE_SHALLOW;                     // ... as is this.
    else
    {                                                  // But using braces is always safer.
        dive_stage = DIVE_SURFACE;
    }
    ...
}
```

**Reasoning**: There is considerable risk associated with the presence of empty statements and single statements that are not surrounded by braces. Code constructs like this are often associated with bugs when nearby code is changed or commented out. This risk is entirely eliminated by the consistent use of braces. The placement of the left brace on the following line allows for easy visual checking for the corresponding right brace.

**Enforcement**: The presence of a left brace after each `if`, `else`, `switch`, `while`, do, and `for` shall be enforced by an automated tool at build time. The same tool or another (such as a code beautifier) shall be used to enforce the alignment of braces.

## 1.4 Parentheses

**Rules**:

a. Do not rely on C's operator precedence rules, as they may not be obvious to those who maintain the code. To aid clarity, use parentheses (and/or break long statements into multiple lines of code) to ensure proper execution order within a sequence of operations.

b. Unless it is a single identifier or constant, each operand of the logical AND (&&) and logical OR (||) operators shall be surrounded by parentheses.

**Example**:

```
if ((depth_in_cm > 0) && (depth_in_cm < MAX_DEPTH))
{
    depth_in_ft = convert_depth_to_ft(depth_in_cm);
}
```

**Reasoning**: The syntax of the C programming language has many operators. The precedence rules that dictate which operators are evaluated before which others are complicated—with over a dozen priority levels—and not always obvious to all programmers. When in doubt it's better to be explicit about what you hope the compiler will do with your calculations.

**Enforcement**: These rules shall be enforced during code reviews.

## 1.5 Common Abbreviations

**Rules**:

a. Abbreviations and acronyms should generally be avoided unless their meanings are widely and consistently understood in the engineering community.

b. A table of project-specific abbreviations and acronyms shall be maintained in a version-controlled document.

**Example**: *Appendix A* contains a sample table of abbreviations and their meanings.

**Reasoning**: Programmers too readily use cryptic abbreviations and acronyms in their code (and in their resumes!). Just because you know what ZYZGXL means today doesn't mean the programmer(s) who have to read/maintain/port your code will later be able to make sense of your cryptic names that reference it.

**Enforcement**: These rules shall be enforced during code reviews.

## 1.6 Casts

**Rules**:

  a. Each cast shall feature an associated comment describing how the code ensures proper behavior across the range of possible values on the right side.

**Example**:

```
int
abs (int arg)
{
    return ((arg < 0) ? -arg : arg);
}

...

    uint16_t sample = adc_read(ADC_CHANNEL_1);

    result = abs((int) sample);              // WARNING: 32-bit int assumed.
```

**Reasoning**: Casting is dangerous. In the example above, unsigned 16-bit "sample" can hold larger positive values than a signed 16-bit integer. In that case, the absolute value will be incorrect as well. Thus there is a possible overflow if int is only 16-bits, which the ISO C standard permits.

**Enforcement**: This rule shall be enforced during code reviews.

## 1.7 Keywords to Avoid

**Rules**:

a. The `auto` keyword shall not be used.

b. The `register` keyword shall not be used.

c. It is a preferred practice to avoid all use of the `goto` keyword. If `goto` is used it shall only jump to a label declared later in the same or an enclosing block.

d. It is a preferred practice to avoid all use of the `continue` keyword.

**Reasoning**: The `auto` keyword is an unnecessary historical feature of the language. The `register` keyword presumes the programmer is smarter than the compiler. There is no compelling reason to use either of these keywords in modern programming practice.

The keywords `goto` and `continue` still serve purposes in the language, but their use too often results in spaghetti code. In particular, the use of `goto` to make jumps orthogonal to the ordinary control flows of the structured programming paradigm is problematic. The occasional use of `goto` to handle an exceptional circumstance is acceptable if it simplifies and clarifies the code.

**Enforcement**: The presence of forbidden keywords in new or modified source code shall be detected and reported via an automated tool at each build. To the extent that the use of `goto` or `continue` is permitted, code reviewers should investigate alternative code structures to improve code maintainability and readability.

## 1.8 Keywords to Frequent

**Rules**:

a. The `static` keyword shall be used to declare all functions and variables that do not need to be visible outside of the module in which they are declared.

b. The `const` keyword shall be used whenever appropriate. Examples include:

   i. To declare variables that should not be changed after initialization,

   ii. To define call-by-reference function parameters that should not be modified (e.g., `char const * param`),

   iii. To define fields in a `struct` or `union` that should not be modified (e.g., in a struct overlay for memory-mapped I/O peripheral registers), and

   iv. As a strongly typed alternative to `#define` for numerical constants.

c. The `volatile` keyword shall be used whenever appropriate. Examples include:

   i. To declare a global variable accessible (by current use or scope) by any interrupt service routine,

   ii. To declare a global variable accessible (by current use or scope) by two or more threads,

   iii. To declare a pointer to a memory-mapped I/O peripheral register set (e.g., `timer_t volatile * const p_timer`), and

   iv. To declare a delay loop counter.

**Example**:
```
typedef struct
{
    uint16_t         count;
    uint16_t         max_count;
    uint16_t const   _unused;    // read-only register
    uint16_t         control;
} timer_reg_t;

timer_reg_t volatile * const p_timer = (timer_reg_t *) HW_TIMER_ADDR;
```

**Reasoning**: C's `static` keyword has several meanings. At the module-level, global variables and functions declared `static` are protected from external use. Heavy-handed use of `static` in this way thus decreases coupling between modules.

The `const` and `volatile` keywords are even more important. The upside of using `const` as much as possible is compiler-enforced protection from unintended writes to data that should be read-only. Proper use of `volatile` eliminates a whole class of difficult-to-detect bugs by preventing compiler optimizations that would eliminate requested reads or writes to variables or registers.[4]

**Enforcement**: These rules shall be enforced during code reviews.

---

[4] Anecdotal evidence suggests that programmers unfamiliar with the `volatile` keyword believe their compiler's optimization feature is more broken than helpful and disable optimization. We believe that the vast majority of embedded systems contain bugs waiting to happen due to missing `volatile` keywords. Such bugs typically manifest themselves as "glitches" or only after changes are made to a "proven" code base.

# 2 Comment Rules

## 2.1 Acceptable Formats

**Rules**:

a. Single-line comments in the C++ style (i.e., preceded by //) are a useful and acceptable alternative to traditional C style comments (i.e., /* ... */).

b. Comments shall never contain the preprocessor tokens /*, //, or \.

c. Code shall never be commented out, even temporarily.

   i. To temporarily disable a block of code, use the preprocessor's conditional compilation feature (e.g., #if 0 ... #endif).

   ii. Any line or block of code that exists specifically to increase the level of debug output information shall be surrounded by #ifndef NDEBUG ... #endif.

**Example**:
```
/* The following code was meant to be part of the build...
...
safety_checker();
...
/* ... but an end of comment character sequence was omitted. */
```

**Reasoning**: Whether intentional or not, nested comments run the risk of confusing source code reviewers about the chunks of the code that will be compiled and run. Our choice of negative-logic NDEBUG is deliberate, as that constant is also associated with disabling the assert() macro. In both cases, the programmer acts to disable the verbose code.

**Enforcement**: The use of only permitted comment formats can be partially enforced by the compiler or static analysis. However, only human code reviewers can tell the difference between commented-out code and comments containing descriptive code snippets.

## 2.2 Locations and Content

**Rules:**

a. All comments shall be written in clear and complete sentences, with proper spelling and grammar and appropriate punctuation.

b. The most useful comments generally precede a block of code that performs one step of a larger algorithm. A blank line shall follow each such code block. The comments in front of the block should be at the same indentation level.

c. Avoid explaining the obvious. Assume the reader knows the C programming language. For example, end-of-line comments should only be used where the meaning of that one line of code may be unclear from the variable and function names and operations alone but where a short comment makes it clear. Specifically, avoid writing unhelpful and redundant comments, e.g., `"numero <<= 2;   // Shift numero left 2 bits."`.

d. The number and length of individual comment blocks shall be proportional to the complexity of the code they describe.

e. Whenever an algorithm or technical detail is defined in an external reference—e.g., a design specification, patent, or textbook—a comment shall include a sufficient reference to the original source to allow a reader of the code to locate the document.

f. Whenever a flow chart or other diagram is needed to sufficiently document the code, the drawing shall be maintained with the source code under version control and the comments should reference the diagram by file name or title.

g. All assumptions shall be spelled out in comments.[5]

h. Each module and function shall be commented in a manner suitable for automatic documentation generation, e.g., via Doxygen.

---

[5] Even better than comments is a set of design-by-contract tests or assertions. See, e.g., barrgroup.com/embedded-systems/how-to/design-by-contract-for-embedded-software.

i. Use the following capitalized comment markers to highlight important issues:

   i. "`WARNING:`" alerts a maintainer there is risk in changing this code. For example, that a delay loop counter's terminal value was determined empirically and may need to change when the code is ported or the optimization level tweaked.

   ii. "`NOTE:`" provides descriptive comments about the "why" of a chunk of code—as distinguished from the "how" usually placed in comments. For example, that a chunk of driver code deviates from the datasheet because there was an errata in the chip. Or that an assumption is being made by the original programmer.

   iii. "`TODO:`" indicates an area of the code is still under construction and explains what remains to be done. When appropriate, an all-caps programmer name or set of initials may be included before the word TODO (e.g., "`MJB TODO:`").

**Example**:

```c
// Step 1: Batten down the hatches.
for (int hatch = 0; hatch < NUM_HATCHES; hatch++)
{
    if (hatch_is_open(hatches[hatch]))
    {
        hatch_close(hatches[hatch]);
    }
}

// Step 2: Raise the mizzenmast.
// TODO: Define mizzenmast driver API.
```

**Reasoning:** Following these rules results in good comments. And good comments correlate with good code. It is a best practice to write the comments before writing the code that implements the behaviors those comments outline.

Unfortunately, it is easy for source code and documentation to drift over time. The best way to prevent this is to keep the documentation as close to the code as possible. Likewise, anytime a question is asked about a section of the code that was previously thought to be clear, you should add a comment addressing that issue nearby.

Doxygen is a useful tool to generate documentation describing the modules, functions, and parameters of an API for its users. However, comments are also still necessary inside the function bodies to reduce the cost of code maintenance.

**Enforcement:** The quality of comments shall be evaluated during code reviews. Code reviewers should verify that comments accurately describe the code and are also clear, concise, and valuable. Automatically generated documentation should be rebuilt each time the software is built.

# 3 White Space Rules

## 3.1 Spaces

**Rules**:

a. Each of the keywords `if`, `while`, `for`, `switch`, and `return` shall be followed by one space when there is additional program text on the same line.

b. Each of the assignment operators =, +=, -=, *=, /=, %=, &=, |=, ^=, ~=, and != shall always be preceded and followed by one space.

c. Each of the binary operators +, -, *, /, %, <, <=, >, >=, ==, !=, <<, >>, &, |, ^, &&, and || shall always be preceded and followed by one space.

d. Each of the unary operators +, -, ++, --, !, and ~, shall be written without a space on the operand side.

e. The pointer operators * and & shall be written with white space on each side within declarations but otherwise without a space on the operand side.

f. The ? and : characters that comprise the ternary operator shall each always be preceded and followed by one space.

g. The structure pointer and structure member operators (-> and ., respectively) shall always be without surrounding spaces.

h. The left and right brackets of the array subscript operator ([ and ]) shall be without surrounding spaces, except as required by another white space rule.

i. Expressions within parentheses shall always have no spaces adjacent to the left and right parenthesis characters.

j. The left and right parentheses of the function call operator shall always be without surrounding spaces, except that the function declaration shall feature one space between the function name and the left parenthesis to allow that one particular mention of the function name to be easily located.

k. Except when at the end of a line, each comma separating function parameters shall always be followed by one space.

l. Each semicolon separating the elements of a *for* statement shall always be followed by one space.

m. Each semicolon shall follow the statement it terminates without a preceding space.

**Example**: See *Appendix D*.

**Reasoning**: In source code, the placement of white space is as important as the placement of text. Good use of white space reduces eyestrain and increases the ability of programmers and reviewers of the code to spot potential bugs.

**Enforcement**: These rules shall be followed by programmers as they work as well as reinforced via a code beautifier, e.g., GNU Indent.

## 3.2 Alignment

**Rules**:

a. The names of variables within a series of declarations shall have their first characters aligned.

b. The names of `struct` and `union` members shall have their first characters aligned.

c. The assignment operators within a block of adjacent assignment statements shall be aligned.

d. The # in a preprocessor directive shall always be located at the start of a line, though the directives themselves may be indented within a `#if` or `#ifdef` sequence.

**Example**:

```
#ifdef USE_UNICODE_STRINGS
#   define BUFFER_BYTES    128
#else
#   define BUFFER_BYTES    64
#endif
...
typedef struct
{
    uint8_t    buffer[BUFFER_BYTES];
    uint8_t    checksum;

} string_t;
```

**Reasoning**: Visual alignment emphasizes similarity. A series of consecutive lines each containing a variable declaration is easily seen and understood as a block of related lines of code. Blank lines and differing alignments should be used as appropriate to visually separate and distinguish unrelated blocks of code that happen to be located in proximity.

**Enforcement**: These rules shall be enforced during code reviews.

## 3.3 Blank Lines

**Rules**:

a. No line of code shall contain more than one statement.

b. There shall be a blank line before and after each natural block of code. Examples of natural blocks of code are loops, `if...else` and `switch` statements, and consecutive declarations.

c. Each source file shall terminate with a comment marking the end of file followed by a blank line.

**Example**: See *Appendix D*.

**Reasoning**: Appropriate placement of white space provides visual separation and thus makes code easier to read and understand, just as the white space areas between paragraphs of this coding standard aid readability. Clearly marking the end of a file is important for human reviewers looking at printouts and the blank line following may be required by some older compilers.

**Enforcement**: These rules shall be enforced during code reviews.

## 3.4 Indentation

**Rules**:

a. Each indentation level should align at a multiple of 4 characters from the start of the line.

b. Within a `switch` statement, the `case` labels shall be aligned; the contents of each case block shall be indented once from there.

c. Whenever a line of code is too long to fit within the maximum line width, indent the second and any subsequent lines in the most readable manner possible.

**Example**:

```
sys_error_handler(int err)
{
    switch (err)
    {
        case ERR_THE_FIRST:
            ...
            break;

        default:
            ...
            break;
    }

    // Purposefully misaligned indentation; see why?
    if ((first_very_long_comparison_here
            && second_very_long_comparison_here)
        || third_very_long_comparison_here)
    {
        ...
    }
}
```

**Reasoning**: Fewer indentation spaces increase the risk of visual confusion while more spaces increases the likelihood of line wraps.

**Enforcement**: A tool, such as a code beautifier, shall be available to programmers to convert indentations of other sizes in an automated manner. This tool shall be used on all new or modified files prior to each build.

## 3.5 Tabs

**Rules**:

    a. The tab character (ASCII 0x09) shall never appear within any source code file.

**Example**:

```
// When tabs are needed inside a string, use the '\t' character.
#define COPYRIGHT   "Copyright (c) 2018 Barr Group.\tAll rights reserved."

// When indents are needed in the source code, align via spaces instead.
void
main (void)
{
        // If not, you can encounter
    // all sorts
        // of weird and
            // uneven
                // alignment of code and comments... across tools.
}
```

**Reasoning**: The width of the tab character varies by text editor and programmer preference, making consistent visual layout a continual source of headaches during code reviews and maintenance.

**Enforcement**: Each programmer should configure his or her code editing tools to insert spaces when the keyboard's TAB key is pressed. The presence of a tab character in new or modified code shall be flagged via an automated scan at each build or code check-in.

## 3.6 Non-Printing Characters

**Rules**:

a. Whenever possible, all source code lines shall end only with the single character 'LF' (ASCII 0x0A), not with the pair 'CR'-'LF' (0x0D 0x0A).

b. The only other non-printable character permitted in a source code file is the form feed character 'FF' (ASCII 0x0C).

**Example**: It's not possible to demonstrate non-printing characters in print.

**Reasoning**: The multi-character sequence 'CR'-'LF' is more likely to cause problems in a multi-platform development environment than the single character 'LF'. One such problem is associated with multi-line preprocessor macros on Unix platforms.

**Enforcement**: Whenever possible, programmer's editors shall be configured to use LF. In addition, an automated tool shall scan all new or modified source code files during each build, replacing each CR-LF sequence with an LF.

# 4 Module Rules

## 4.1 *Naming Conventions*

**Rules**:

a. All module names shall consist entirely of lowercase letters, numbers, and underscores. No spaces shall appear within the module's header and source file names.

b. All module names shall be unique in their first 8 characters and end with suffices `.h` and `.c` for the header and source file names, respectively.

c. No module's header file name shall share the name of a header file from the C Standard Library or C++ Standard Library. For example, modules shall not be named "`stdio`" or "`math`".

d. Any module containing a `main()` function shall have the word "`main`" as part of its source file name.

**Example**: See *Appendix D*.

**Reasoning**: Multi-platform development environments (e.g., Unix and Windows) are the norm rather than the exception. Mixed case names can cause problems across operating systems and are also error prone due to the possibility of similarly-named but differently-capitalized files becoming confused by human programmers.

The inclusion of "`main`" in a file name is an aid to code maintainers that has proven useful in projects with multiple software configurations.

**Enforcement**: An automated tool shall confirm that all file names that are part of a build are consistent with these rules.

## 4.2 Header Files

**Rules**:

a. There shall always be precisely one header file for each source file and they shall always have the same root name.

b. Each header file shall contain a preprocessor guard against multiple inclusion, as shown in the example below.[6]

c. The header file shall identify only the procedures, constants, and data types (via prototypes or macros, #define, and typedefs, respectively) about which it is strictly necessary for other modules to be informed.

   i. It is a preferred practice that no variable ever be declared (via extern) in a header file.

   ii. No storage for any variable shall be allocated in a header file.

d. No public header file shall contain a #include of any private header file.

**Example**:

```
#ifndef ADC_H
#define ADC_H
...
#endif /* ADC_H */
```

**Reasoning**: The C language standard gives all variables and functions global scope by default. The downside of this is unnecessary (and dangerous) coupling between modules. To reduce inter-module coupling, keep as many procedures, constants, data types, and variables as possible privately hidden within a module's source file.

See also *What Belongs in a C .h Header File?*:

embeddedgurus.com/barr-code/2010/11/what-belongs-in-a-c-h-header-file/

**Enforcement**: These rules shall be enforced during code reviews.

---

[6] The preprocessor directive "#pragma once" has the same purpose but is non-portable.

## 4.3 Source Files

**Rules:**

a. Each source file shall include only the behaviors appropriate to control one "entity". Examples of entities include encapsulated data types, active objects, peripheral drivers (e.g., for a UART), and communication protocols or layers (e.g., ARP).

b. Each source file shall be comprised of some or all of the following sections, in the order listed: comment block; include statements; data type, constant, and macro definitions; static data declarations; private function prototypes; public function bodies; then private function bodies.

c. Each source file shall always #include the header file of the same name (e.g., file adc.c should #include "adc.h"), to allow the compiler to confirm that each public function and its prototype match.

d. Absolute paths shall not be used in include file names.

e. Each source file shall be free of unused include files.

f. No source file shall #include another source file.

**Example:** See *Appendix D*.

**Reasoning:** The purpose and internal layout of a source file module should be clear to all who maintain it. For example, the public functions are generally of most interest and thus appear ahead of the private functions they call. Of critical importance is that every function declaration be matched by the compiler against its prototype.

**Enforcement:** Most static analysis tools can be configured to check for include files that are not actually used. The other rules shall be enforced during code reviews.

## 4.4 File Templates

**Rules**:

a. A set of templates for header files and source files shall be maintained at the project level.

**Example**: See *Appendix B* and *Appendix C* for sample file templates.

**Reasoning**: Starting each new file from a template ensures consistency in file header comment blocks and ensures inclusion of appropriate copyright notices.

**Enforcement**: The consistency of file formats shall be enforced during code reviews.

# 5 Data Type Rules

## 5.1 Naming Conventions

**Rules**:

a. The names of all new data types, including structures, unions, and enumerations, shall consist only of lowercase characters and internal underscores and end with '_t'.

b. All new structures, unions, and enumerations shall be named via a `typedef`.

c. The name of all public data types shall be prefixed with their module name and an underscore.

**Example**:

```
typedef struct
{
    uint16_t  count;
    uint16_t  max_count;
    uint16_t  _unused;
    uint16_t  control;

} timer_reg_t;
```

**Reasoning**: Data type names and variable names are often appropriately similar. For example, a set of timer control registers in a peripheral calls out to be named '`timer_reg`'. To distinguish the structure definition that defines the register layout, it is valuable to create a new type with a distinct name, such as '`timer_reg_t`'. If necessary this same type could then be used to create a shadow copy of the timer registers, say called '`timer_reg_shadow`'.

**Enforcement**: An automated tool shall scan new or modified source code prior to each build to ensure that the keywords `struct`, `union`, and `enum` are used only within `typedef` statements or in anonymous declarations. Code reviews shall be used to enforce the naming rules for new types.

## 5.2 Fixed-Width Integers

**Rules**:

a. Whenever the width, in bits or bytes, of an integer value matters in the program, one of the fixed width data types shall be used in place of `char`, `short`, `int`, `long`, or `long long`. The signed and unsigned fixed-width integer types shall be as shown in the table below.

| Integer Width | Signed Type | Unsigned Type |
|---|---|---|
| 8 bits | int8_t | uint8_t |
| 16 bits | int16_t | uint16_t |
| 32 bits | int32_t | uint32_t |
| 64 bits | int64_t | uint64_t |

b. The keywords `short` and `long` shall not be used.

c. Use of the keyword `char` shall be restricted to the declaration of and operations concerning strings.

**Example**: See *Appendix D*.

**Reasoning**: The C90 standard purposefully allowed for implementation-defined widths for `char`, `short`, `int`, `long`, and `long long` types, which has resulted in code portability problems. The C99 standard did not resolve this but did introduce the type names shown in the table, which are defined in the `stdint.h` header file.

See also *Portable Fixed-Width Integers in C*:

barrgroup.com/embedded-systems/how-to/c-fixed-width-integers-c99

In the absence of a C99-compatible compiler, it is acceptable to define the set of fixed-width types in the table above as typedefs built from underlying types. If this is necessary, be sure to use compile-time checking (e.g., static assertions).

**Enforcement**: At every build an automated tool shall flag any use of keywords `short` or `long`. Compliance with the other rules shall be checked during code reviews.

## 5.3 Signed and Unsigned Integers

**Rules**:

a. Bit-fields shall not be defined within `signed` integer types.

b. None of the bitwise operators (i.e., &, |, ~, ^, <<, and >>) shall be used to manipulate signed integer data.

c. Signed integers shall not be combined with unsigned integers in comparisons or expressions. In support of this, decimal constants meant to be unsigned should be declared with a 'u' at the end.

**Example**:

```
uint16_t   unsigned_a = 6u;
int16_t    signed_b   = -9;

if (unsigned_a + signed_b < 4)
{
    // Execution of this block appears reliably logical, as -9 + 6 is -3
    ...
}
// ... but compilers with 16-bit int may legally perform (0xFFFF - 9) + 6.
```

**Reasoning**: Several details of the manipulation of binary data within signed integer containers are implementation-defined behaviors of the ISO C standards. Additionally, the results of mixing signed and unsigned integers can lead to data-dependent outcomes like the one in the code above.[7] Beware that the use of C99's fixed-width integer types does not by itself prevent such defects.

**Enforcement**: Static analysis tools can be used to detect violations of these rules.

---

[7] [MISRA-C] describes problems that can arise from mixing C's "essential types" at length in its Appendix C and Appendix D.

## 5.4 Floating Point

**Rules**:

a. Avoid the use of floating point constants and variables whenever possible. Fixed-point math may be an alternative.

b. When floating point calculations are necessary:

   i. Use the C99 type names `float32_t`, `float64_t`, and `float128_t`.

   ii. Append an 'f' to all single-precision constants (e.g., `pi = 3.141592f`).

   iii. Ensure that the compiler supports double precision, if your math depends on it.

   iv. Never test for equality or inequality of floating point values.

   v. Always invoke the `isfinite()` macro to check that prior calculations have resulted in neither `INFINITY` nor `NAN`.

**Example**:

```
#include <limits.h>
#if (DBL_DIG < 10)   // Ensure the compiler supports double precision.
#   error "Double precision is not available!"
#endif
```

**Reasoning**: A large number of risks of defects stem from incorrect use of floating point arithmetic.[8] By default, C promotes all floating-point constants to `double` precision, which may be inefficient or unsupported on the target platform. However, many microcontrollers do not have any hardware support for floating point math. The compiler may not warn of these incompatibilities, instead performing the requested numerical operations by linking in a large (typically a few kilobytes of code) and slow (numerous instruction cycles per operation) floating-point emulation library.

**Enforcement**: These rules shall be enforced during code reviews.

---

[8] [CERT-C] has an explanation of these issues in its Chapter 5.

## 5.5 Structures and Unions

**Rules**:

a. Appropriate care shall be taken to prevent the compiler from inserting padding bytes within `struct` or `union` types used to communicate to or from a peripheral or over a bus or network to another processor.

b. Appropriate care shall be taken to prevent the compiler from altering the intended order of the bits within bit-fields.

**Example**:

```
typedef struct
{
    uint16_t  count;                    // offset 0
    uint16_t  max_count;                // offset 2
    uint16_t  _unused;                  // offset 4

    uint16_t  enable      : 2;          // offset 6 bits 15-14
    uint16_t  b_interrupt : 1;          // offset 6 bit  13
    uint16_t  _unused1    : 7;          // offset 6 bits 12-6
    uint16_t  b_complete  : 1;          // offset 6 bit  5
    uint16_t  _unused2    : 4;          // offset 6 bits 4-1
    uint16_t  b_periodic  : 1;          // offset 6 bit  0

} timer_reg_t;

// Preprocessor check of timer register layout byte count.
#if ((8 != sizeof(timer_reg_t))
#   error "timer_reg_t struct size incorrect (expected 8 bytes)"
#endif
```

## Embedded C Coding Standard

**Reasoning**: Owing to differences across processor families and loose definitions in the ISO C language standards, there is a tremendous amount of implementation-defined behavior in the area of structures and unions. Bit-fields, in particular, suffer from severe portability problems, including the lack of a standard bit ordering and no official support for the fixed-width integer types they so often call out to be used with. The methods available to check the layout of such data structures include static assertions or other compile-time checks as well as the use of preprocessor directives, e.g., to select one of two competing struct layouts based on the compiler.

**Enforcement**: These rules shall be enforced during code reviews.

## 5.6 Booleans

**Rules**:

a. Boolean variables shall be declared as type `bool`.

b. Non-Boolean values shall be converted to Boolean via use of relational operators (e.g., < or !=), not via casts.

**Example**:

```
#include <stdbool.h>
...

    bool b_in_motion = (0 != speed_in_mph);
```

**Reasoning**: The C90 standard did not define a data type for Boolean variables and C programmers have widely treated any non-zero integer value as true. The C99 language standard is backward compatible with this old style, but also introduced a new data type for Boolean variables along with new constants `true` and `false` in the `stdbool.h` header file.

**Enforcement**: These rules shall be enforced during code reviews.

# 6 Procedure Rules

## 6.1 Naming Conventions

**Rules**:

a. No procedure shall have a name that is a keyword of any standard version of the C or C++ programming language. Restricted names include `interrupt`, `inline`, `class`, `true`, `false`, `public`, `private`, `friend`, `protected`, and many others.

b. No procedure shall have a name that overlaps a function in the C Standard Library. Examples of such names include `strlen`, `atoi`, and `memset`.

c. No procedure shall have a name that begins with an underscore.

d. No procedure name shall be longer than 31 characters.

e. No function name shall contain any uppercase letters.

f. No macro name shall contain any lowercase letters.

g. Underscores shall be used to separate words in procedure names.

h. Each procedure's name shall be descriptive of its purpose. Note that procedures encapsulate the "actions" of a program and thus benefit from the use of verbs in their names (e.g., `adc_read()`); this "noun-verb" word ordering is recommended. Alternatively, procedures may be named according to the question they answer (e.g., `led_is_on()`).

i. The names of all public functions shall be prefixed with their module name and an underscore (e.g., `sensor_read()`).

**Example**: See *Appendix D*.

**Reasoning**: Good function names make reviewing and maintaining code easier (and thus cheaper). The data (variables) in programs are nouns. Functions manipulate data and are thus verbs. The use of module prefixes is in keeping with the important goal of encapsulation and helps avoid procedure name overlaps.

**Enforcement**: Compliance with these naming rules shall be established in the detailed design phase and be enforced during code reviews.

## 6.2 Functions

**Rules**:

a. All reasonable effort shall be taken to keep the length of each function limited to one printed page, or a maximum of 100 lines.

b. Whenever possible, all functions shall be made to start at the top of a printed page, except when several small functions can fit onto a single page.[9]

c. It is a preferred practice that all functions shall have just one exit point and it shall be via a `return` at the bottom of the function.

d. A prototype shall be declared for each public function in the module header file.

e. All private functions shall be declared `static`.

f. Each parameter shall be explicitly declared and meaningfully named.

---

[9] One way this can be accomplished is to insert a form feed character 'FF' (ASCII 0x0C) at the beginning of the first line on the comment block that precedes the function definition.

**Example**:

```c
int
state_change (int event)
{
    int result = ERROR;

    if (EVENT_A == event)
    {
        result = STATE_A;
    }
    else
    {
        result = STATE_B;
    }
    return (result);
}
```

**Reasoning**: Code reviews take place at the function level and often on paper. Each function should thus ideally be visible on a single printed page, so that flipping papers back and forth does not distract the reviewers.

Multiple `return` statements should be used only when it improves the readability of the code.

**Enforcement**: Compliance with these rules shall be checked during code reviews.

## 6.3 Function-Like Macros

**Rules**:

a. Parameterized macros shall not be used if a function can be written to accomplish the same behavior.

b. If parameterized macros are used for some reason, these rules apply:

   i. Surround the entire macro body with parentheses.

   ii. Surround each use of a parameter with parentheses.

   iii. Use each parameter no more than once, to avoid unintended side effects.

   iv. Never include a transfer of control (e.g., `return` keyword).

**Example**:

```c
// Don't do this ...
#define MAX(A, B)    ((A) > (B) ? (A) : (B))

// ... when you can do this instead.
inline int max(int num1, int num2)
```

**Reasoning**: There are a lot of risks associated with the use of preprocessor defines, and many of them relate to the creation of parameterized macros. The extensive use of parentheses (as shown in the example) is important, but does not eliminate the unintended double increment possibility of a call such as `MAX(i++, j++)`. Other risks of macro misuse include comparison of signed and unsigned data or any test of floating-point data. Making matters worse, macros are invisible at run-time and thus impossible to step into within the debugger.

Where performance is important, note that C99 added C++'s `inline` keyword.

**Enforcement**: These rules shall be enforced during code reviews.

## 6.4 Threads of Execution

**Rules:**

a. All functions that encapsulate threads of execution (a.k.a., tasks, processes) shall be given names ending with "`_thread`" (or "`_task`", "`_process`").

**Example:**

```
void
alarm_thread (void * p_data)
{
    alarm_t  alarm = ALARM_NONE;
    int      err   = OS_NO_ERR;

    for (;;)
    {
        alarm = OSMboxPend(alarm_mbox, &err);
        // Process alarm here.
    }
}
```

**Reasoning:** Each task in a real-time operating system (RTOS) is like a mini-`main()`, typically running forever in an infinite loop. It is valuable to easily identify these important, asynchronous functions during code reviews and debugging sessions.

**Enforcement:** This rule shall be followed during the detailed design phase and enforced during code reviews.

## 6.5 Interrupt Service Routines

**Rules**:

a. Interrupt service routines (ISRs) are not ordinary functions. The compiler must be informed that the function is an ISR by way of a `#pragma` or compiler-specific keyword, such as "`__interrupt`".

b. All functions that implement ISRs shall be given names ending with "`_isr`".

c. To ensure that ISRs are not inadvertently called from other parts of the software (they may corrupt the CPU and call stack if this happens), each ISR function shall be declared `static` and/or be located at the end of the associated driver module as permitted by the target platform.

d. A stub or default ISR shall be installed in the vector table at the location of all unexpected or otherwise unhandled interrupt sources. Each such stub could attempt to disable future interrupts of the same type, say at the interrupt controller, and `assert()`.

**Example**:

```
#pragma irq_entry
void
timer_isr (void)
{
    uint8_t static  prev = 0x00;                // prev button states
    uint8_t         curr = *gp_button_reg;      // curr button states

    // Compare current and previous button states.
    g_debounced |= (prev & curr);               // record all closes
    g_debounced &= (prev | curr);               // record all opens

    // Save current pin states for next interrupt
    prev = curr;

    // Acknowledge timer interrupt at hardware, if necessary.
}
```

**Reasoning**: An ISR is an extension of the hardware. By definition, it and the straight-line code are asynchronous to each other. If they share global variables or registers, those singleton objects must be protected via interrupt disables in the straight-line code. The ISR must not get hung up inside the operating system or waiting for a variable or register to change value.

Note that platform-specific ISR installation steps vary and may require ISRs functions to have prototypes and in other ways be visible to at least one other function.

Although stub interrupt handlers don't directly prevent defects, they can certainly make a system more robust in real-world operating conditions.

**Enforcement**: These rules shall be enforced during code reviews.

# 7 Variable Rules

## 7.1 Naming Conventions

**Rules**:

a. No variable shall have a name that is a keyword of C, C++, or any other well-known extension of the C programming language, including specifically K&R C and C99. Restricted names include `interrupt`, `inline`, `restrict`, `class`, `true`, `false`, `public`, `private`, `friend`, and `protected`.

b. No variable shall have a name that overlaps with a variable name from the C Standard Library (e.g., `errno`).

c. No variable shall have a name that begins with an underscore.

d. No variable name shall be longer than 31 characters.

e. No variable name shall be shorter than 3 characters, including loop counters.

f. No variable name shall contain any uppercase letters.

g. No variable name shall contain any numeric value that is called out elsewhere, such as the number of elements in an array or the number of bits in the underlying type.

h. Underscores shall be used to separate words in variable names.

i. Each variable's name shall be descriptive of its purpose.

j. The names of any global variables shall begin with the letter 'g'. For example, `g_zero_offset`.

k. The names of any pointer variables shall begin with the letter 'p'. For example, `p_led_reg`.

l. The names of any pointer-to-pointer variables shall begin with the letters 'pp'. For example, `pp_vector_table`.

m. The names of all integer variables containing Boolean information (including 0 vs. non-zero) shall begin with the letter 'b' and phrased as the question they answer. For example, `b_done_yet` or `b_is_buffer_full`.

n. The names of any variables representing non-pointer handles for objects, e.g., file handles, shall begin with the letter 'h'. For example, `h_input_file`.

o. In the case of a variable name requiring multiple of the above prefixes, the order of their inclusion before the first underscore shall be [g][p | pp][b | h].

**Example**: See *Appendix D*.

**Reasoning**: The base rules are adopted to maximize code portability across compilers. Many C compilers recognize differences only in the first 31 characters in a variable's name and reserve names beginning with an underscore for internal names.

The other rules are meant to highlight risks and ensure consistent proper use of variables. For example, all code relating to the use of global variables and other singleton objects, including peripheral registers, needs to be carefully considered to ensure there can be no race conditions or data corruptions via asynchronous writes.

**Enforcement**: These rules shall be enforced during code reviews.

## 7.2 Initialization

**Rules**:

a. All variables shall be initialized before use.

b. It is preferable to define local variables as you need them, rather than all at the top of a function.

c. If project- or file-global variables are used, their definitions shall be grouped together and placed at the top of a source code file.

d. Any pointer variable lacking an initial address shall be initialized to NULL.

**Example**:

```
uint32_t  g_array[NUM_ROWS][NUM_COLS] = { ... };
...

    for (int col = 0; col < NUM_COLS; col++)
    {
        g_array[row][col] = ...;
    }
```

**Reasoning**: Too many programmers assume the C run-time will watch out for them, e.g., by zeroing the value of uninitialized variables on system startup. This is a bad assumption, which can prove dangerous in a mission-critical system. For readability reasons it is better to declare local variables as close as possible to their first use,[10] which C99 makes possible by incorporating that earlier feature of C++.

**Enforcement**: An automated tool shall scan all of the source code prior to each build, to warn about variables used prior to initialization; static analysis tools can do this. The remainder of these rules shall be enforced during code reviews.

---

[10] [Uwano] describes back-and-forth code review eye movements that demonstrate the value of placing variable declarations as close as possible to the code that first references them.

# 8 Statement Rules

## 8.1 Variable Declarations

**Rules**:

a. The comma operator (`,`) shall not be used within variable declarations.

**Example**:

```
char * x, y;   // Was y intended to be a pointer also?  Don't do this.
```

**Reasoning**: The cost of placing each declaration on a line of its own is low. By contrast, the risk that either the compiler or a maintainer will misunderstand your intentions is high.

**Enforcement**: This rule shall be enforced during code reviews.

## 8.2 Conditional Statements

**Rules**:

a. It is a preferred practice that the shortest (measured in lines of code) of the `if` and `else if` clauses should be placed first.

b. Nested `if...else` statements shall not be deeper than two levels. Use function calls or `switch` statements to reduce complexity and aid understanding.

c. Assignments shall not be made within an `if` or `else if` test.

d. Any `if` statement with an `else if` clause shall end with an `else` clause.[11]

**Example**:

```
if (NULL == p_object)
{
    result = ERR_NULL_PTR;
}
else if (p_object = malloc(sizeof(object_t)))  // No assignments!
{
    ...
}
else
{
    // Normal processing steps, which require many lines of code.
    ...
}
```

**Reasoning**: Long clauses can distract the human eye from the decision-path logic. By putting the shorter clause earlier, the decision path becomes easier to follow. (And easier to follow is always good for reducing bugs.) Deeply nested `if...else` statements are a sure sign of a complex and fragile state machine implementation; there is always a safer and more readable way to do the same thing.

**Enforcement**: These rules shall be enforced during code reviews.

---

[11] This is the equivalent of requiring a `default` case in every switch statement.

## 8.3 Switch Statements

**Rules**:

a. The `break` for each `case` shall be indented to align with the associated `case`, rather than with the contents of the case code block.

b. All `switch` statements shall contain a `default` block.

c. Any `case` designed to fall through to the next shall be commented to clearly explain the absence of the corresponding `break`.

**Example**:

```
switch (err)
{
  case ERR_A:
    ...
  break;

  case ERR_B:
    ...
  // Also perform the steps for ERR_C.
  case ERR_C:
    ...
  break;

  default:
    ...
  break;
}
```

**Reasoning**: C's `switch` statements are powerful constructs, but prone to errors such as omitted `break` statements and unhandled cases. By aligning the `case` labels with their `break` statements it is easier to spot a missing `break`.

**Enforcement**: These rules shall be enforced during code reviews.

## 8.4 Loops

**Rules**:

a. Magic numbers shall not be used as the initial value or in the endpoint test of a `while`, `do...while`, or `for` loop.[12]

b. With the exception of the initialization of a loop counter in the first clause of a `for` statement and the change to the same variable in the third, no assignment shall be made in any loop's controlling expression.

c. Infinite loops shall be implemented via controlling expression `for (;;)`.[13]

d. Each loop with an empty body shall feature a set of braces enclosing a comment to explain why nothing needs to be done until after the loop terminates.

**Example**:

```
// Why would anyone bury a magic number (e.g., "100") in their code?
for (int row = 0; row < 100; row++)
{
    // Descriptively-named constants prevent defects and aid readability.
    for (int col = 0; col < NUM_COLS; col++)
    {
        ...
    }
}
```

**Reasoning**: It is always important to synchronize the number of loop iterations to the size of the underlying data structure. Doing this via a descriptively-named constant prevents defects that result when changes in one part of the code, such as the dimension of an array, are not matched in other areas of the code.

**Enforcement**: These rules shall be enforced during code reviews.

---

[12] Note that the `sizeof` macro is a theoretically handy way to dimension an array but that this method does not work when you pass a pointer to the array instead of the array itself.

[13] Kernighan & Ritchie long ago recommended `for (;;)`, which has the additional benefit of insuring against the visually-confusing defect of a `while (l);` referencing a variable 'l'.

## 8.5 Jumps

**Rules**:

a. The use of `goto` statements shall be restricted as per Rule 1.7.c.

b. C Standard Library functions `abort()`, `exit()`, `setjmp()`, and `longjmp()` shall not be used.

**Reasoning**: Algorithms that utilize jumps to move the instruction pointer can and should be rewritten in a manner that is more readable and thus easier to maintain.

**Enforcement**: These rules shall be enforced by an automated scan of all modified or new modules for inappropriate use of forbidden tokens. To the extent that the use of `goto` is permitted, code reviewers should investigate alternative code structures to improve code maintainability and readability.

## 8.6 Equivalence Tests

**Rules**:

a. When evaluating the equality of a variable against a constant, the constant shall always be placed to the left of the equal-to operator (==).

**Example**:

```
if (NULL == p_object)
{
    return (ERR_NULL_PTR);
}
```

**Reasoning**: It is always desirable to detect possible typos and as many other coding defects as possible at compile-time. Defect discovery in later phases is not guaranteed and often also more costly. By following this rule, any compiler will reliably detect erroneous attempts to assign (i.e., = instead of ==) a new value to a constant.

**Enforcement**: Many compilers can be configured to warn about suspicious assignments (i.e., located where comparisons are more typical). However, ultimate responsibility for enforcement of this rule falls to code reviewers.

# Appendix A: Table of Abbreviations

The following abbreviations and acronyms are accepted for use in source code without local explanation.

| Abbreviation | Meaning |
| --- | --- |
| adc | analog-to-digital converter |
| avg | average |
| b_ | Boolean |
| buf | buffer |
| cfg | configuration |
| curr | current (item in a list) |
| dac | digital-to-analog converter |
| ee | EEPROM |
| err | error |
| g_ | global |
| gpio | general-purpose I/O pins |
| h_ | handle (to) |
| init | initialize |
| io | input/output |
| isr | interrupt service routine |
| lcd | liquid crystal display |
| led | light-emitting diode |
| max | maximum |
| mbox | mailbox |
| mgr | manager |
| min | minimum |

| | |
|---|---|
| msec | millisecond[14] |
| msg | message |
| next | next (item in a list) |
| nsec | nanosecond |
| num | number (of) |
| p_ | pointer (to) |
| pp_ | pointer to a pointer (to) |
| prev | previous (item in a list) |
| prio | priority |
| pwm | pulse width modulation |
| q | queue |
| reg | register |
| rx | receive |
| sem | semaphore |
| str | string (null terminated) |
| sync | synchronize |
| temp | temperature |
| tmp | temporary |
| tx | transmit |
| usec | microsecond |

---

[14] Note that second(s) shall not be abbreviated, nor minute, hour, day, week, month, or year. Among other things, this rule eliminates conflict between minute and minimum (for "min").

# Appendix B: Header File Template

```
/** @file module.h
 *
 * @brief A description of the module's purpose.
 *
 * @par
 * COPYRIGHT NOTICE: (c) 2018 Barr Group.  All rights reserved.
 */

#ifndef MODULE_H
#define MODULE_H

int8_t max8(int8_t num1, int8_t num2);

#endif /* MODULE_H */

/*** end of file ***/
```

# Appendix C: Source File Template

```c
/** @file module.c
 *
 * @brief A description of the module's purpose.
 *
 * @par
 * COPYRIGHT NOTICE: (c) 2018 Barr Group.  All rights reserved.
 */

#include <stdint.h>
#include <stdbool.h>

#include "module.h"

/*!
 * @brief Identify the larger of two 8-bit integers.
 *
 * @param[in] num1   The first number to be compared.
 * @param[in] num2   The second number to be compared.
 *
 * @return The value of the larger number.
 */
int8_t
max8 (int8_t num1, int8_t num2)
{
    return ((num1 > num2) ? num1 : num2);
}

/*** end of file ***/
```

# Appendix D: Example Program

```c
/** @file crc.h
 *
 * @brief Compact CRC library for embedded systems for CRC-CCITT, CRC-16, CRC-32.
 *
 * @par
 * COPYRIGHT NOTICE: (c) 2000, 2018 Michael Barr.  This software is placed in the
 * public domain and may be used for any purpose.  However, this notice must not
 * be changed or removed.  No warranty is expressed or implied by the publication
 * or distribution of this source code.
 */

#ifndef CRC_H
#define CRC_H


// Compile-time selection of the desired CRC algorithm.
//
#if defined(CRC_CCITT)

#define CRC_NAME    "CRC-CCITT"
typedef uint16_t    crc_t;

#elif defined(CRC_16)

#define CRC_NAME    "CRC-16"
typedef uint16_t    crc_t;

#elif defined(CRC_32)

#define CRC_NAME    "CRC-32"
typedef uint32_t    crc_t;

#else

#error "One of CRC_CCITT, CRC_16, or CRC_32 must be #define'd."

#endif
```

```c
// Public API functions provided by the Compact CRC library.
//
void    crc_init(void);
crc_t   crc_slow(uint8_t const * const p_message, int n_bytes);
crc_t   crc_fast(uint8_t const * const p_message, int n_bytes);


#endif /* CRC_H */

/*** end of file ***/
```

```c
/** @file crc.c
 *
 * @brief Compact CRC generator for embedded systems, with brute force and table-
 * driven algorithm options.  Supports CRC-CCITT, CRC-16, and CRC-32 standards.
 *
 * @par
 * COPYRIGHT NOTICE: (c) 2000, 2018 Michael Barr.  This software is placed in the
 * public domain and may be used for any purpose.  However, this notice must not
 * be changed or removed.  No warranty is expressed or implied by the publication
 * or distribution of this source code.
 */

#include <stdint.h>

#include "crc.h"


// Algorithmic parameters based on CRC elections made in crc.h.
//
#define BITS_PER_BYTE       8
#define WIDTH               (BITS_PER_BYTE * sizeof(crc_t))
#define TOPBIT              (1 << (WIDTH - 1))

// Allocate storage for the byte-wide CRC lookup table.
//
#define CRC_TABLE_SIZE      256
static crc_t  g_crc_table[CRC_TABLE_SIZE];
```

```c
// Further algorithmic configuration to support the selected CRC standard.
//
#if defined(CRC_CCITT)

#define POLYNOMIAL              ((crc_t) 0x1021)
#define INITIAL_REMAINDER       ((crc_t) 0xFFFF)
#define FINAL_XOR_VALUE         ((crc_t) 0x0000)
#define REFLECT_DATA(X)         (X)
#define REFLECT_REMAINDER(X)    (X)

#elif defined(CRC_16)

#define POLYNOMIAL              ((crc_t) 0x8005)
#define INITIAL_REMAINDER       ((crc_t) 0x0000)
#define FINAL_XOR_VALUE         ((crc_t) 0x0000)
#define REFLECT_DATA(X)         ((uint8_t) reflect((X), BITS_PER_BYTE))
#define REFLECT_REMAINDER(X)    ((crc_t) reflect((X), WIDTH))

#elif defined(CRC_32)

#define POLYNOMIAL              ((crc_t) 0x04C11DB7)
#define INITIAL_REMAINDER       ((crc_t) 0xFFFFFFFF)
#define FINAL_XOR_VALUE         ((crc_t) 0xFFFFFFFF)
#define REFLECT_DATA(X)         ((uint8_t) reflect((X), BITS_PER_BYTE))
#define REFLECT_REMAINDER(X)    ((crc_t) reflect((X), WIDTH))

#endif
```

```c
/*!
 * @brief Compute the reflection of a set of data bits around its center.
 * @param[in] data  The data bits to be reflected.
 * @param[in] num2  The number of bits.
 * @return The reflected data.
 */
static uint32_t
reflect (uint32_t data, uint8_t n_bits)
{
    uint32_t  reflection = 0x00000000;


    // NOTE: For efficiency sake, n_bits is not verified to be <= 32.

    // Reflect the data about the center bit.
    //
    for (uint8_t bit = 0; bit < n_bits; ++bit)
    {
        // If the LSB bit is set, set the reflection of it.
        //
        if (data & 0x01)
        {
            reflection |= (1 << ((n_bits - 1) - bit));
        }

        data = (data >> 1);
    }

    return (reflection);

}   /* reflect() */
```

```c
/*!
 * @brief Initialize the lookup table for byte-by-byte CRC acceleration.
 *
 * @par
 * This function must be run before crc_fast() or the table stored in ROM.
 */
void
crc_init (void)
{
    // Compute the remainder of each possible dividend.
    //
    for (crc_t dividend = 0; dividend < CRC_TABLE_SIZE; ++dividend)
    {
        // Start with the dividend followed by zeros.
        //
        crc_t remainder = dividend << (WIDTH - BITS_PER_BYTE);

        // Perform modulo-2 division, a bit at a time.
        //
        for (int bit = BITS_PER_BYTE; bit > 0; --bit)
        {
            // Try to divide the current data bit.
            //
            if (remainder & TOPBIT)
            {
                remainder = (remainder << 1) ^ POLYNOMIAL;
            }
            else
            {
                remainder = (remainder << 1);
            }
        }

        // Store the result into the table.
        //
        g_crc_table[dividend] = remainder;
    }

}   /* crc_init() */
```

```c
/*!
 * @brief Compute the CRC of an array of bytes, bit-by-bit.
 * @param[in] p_message  A pointer to the array of data bytes to be CRC'd.
 * @param[in] n_bytes    The number of bytes in the array of data.
 * @return The CRC of the array of data.
 */
crc_t
crc_slow (uint8_t const * const p_message, int n_bytes)
{
    crc_t    remainder = INITIAL_REMAINDER;

    // Perform modulo-2 division, one byte at a time.
    //
    for (int byte = 0; byte < n_bytes; ++byte)
    {
        // Bring the next byte into the remainder.
        //
        remainder ^= (REFLECT_DATA(p_message[byte]) << (WIDTH - BITS_PER_BYTE));

        // Perform modulo-2 division, one bit at a time.
        //
        for (int bit = BITS_PER_BYTE; bit > 0; --bit)
        {
            // Try to divide the current data bit.
            //
            if (remainder & TOPBIT)
            {
                remainder = (remainder << 1) ^ POLYNOMIAL;
            }
            else
            {
                remainder = (remainder << 1);
            }
        }
    }

    // The final remainder is the CRC result.
    //
    return (REFLECT_REMAINDER(remainder) ^ FINAL_XOR_VALUE);

}   /* crc_slow() */
```

```c
/*!
 * @brief Compute the CRC of an array of bytes, byte-by-byte.
 * @param[in] p_message  A pointer to the array of data bytes to be CRC'd.
 * @param[in] n_bytes    The number of bytes in the array of data.
 * @return The CRC of the array of data.
 */
crc_t
crc_fast (uint8_t const * const p_message, int n_bytes)
{
    crc_t remainder = INITIAL_REMAINDER;

    // Divide the message by the polynomial, a byte at a time.
    //
    for (int byte = 0; byte < n_bytes; ++byte)
    {
        uint8_t data = REFLECT_DATA(p_message[byte]) ^
                            (remainder >> (WIDTH - BITS_PER_BYTE));
        remainder = g_crc_table[data] ^ (remainder << BITS_PER_BYTE);
    }

    // The final remainder is the CRC.
    //
    return (REFLECT_REMAINDER(remainder) ^ FINAL_XOR_VALUE);
}   /* crc_fast() */

/*** end of file ***/
```

# Bibliography

[Barr]          Barr, Michael. "Programming Embedded Systems in C and C++." O'Reilly, 1999.

[C90]           "ISO/IEC9899:1990, Programming Languages – C," ISO, 1990.

[C99]           "ISO/IEC9899:1999, Programming Languages – C," ISO, 1999.

[CERT-C]        Seacord, Robert C. "The CERT C Coding Standard, Second Edition." Pearson, 2014.

[Harbison]      Harbison III, Samuel P. and Guy L. Steele, Jr. "C: A Reference Manual, Fifth Edition." Prentice Hall, 2002.

[Hatton]        Hatton, Les. "Safer C: Developing Software for High-Integrity and Safety-Critical Systems." McGraw-Hill, 1994.

[Holub]         Holub, Allen I. "Enough Rope to Shoot Yourself in the Foot: Rules for C and C++ Programming." McGraw-Hill, 1995.

[IEC61508]      "Functional Safety of Electrical/Electronic/Programmable Electronic Safety-Related Systems," International Electromechanical Commission, 1998-2000.

[Koenig]        Koenig, Andrew. "C Traps and Pitfalls." Addison-Wesley, 1988.

[Loudon]        Loudon, Kyle. "C++ Pocket Reference." O'Reilly, 2003.

[MISRA-C]       "MISRA C:2012 Guidelines for the use of the C language in critical systems," MIRA, March 2013.

[MISRA-C++]     "MISRA C++ Guidelines for the use of the C++ language in critical systems," MIRA, June 2008.

[Prinz]         Prinz, Peter and Ulla Kirch-Prinz. "C Pocket Reference." O'Reilly, 2003.

[Sutter]        Sutter, Herb and Andrei Alexandrescu. "C++ Coding Standards: 101 Rules, Guidelines, and Best Practices." Pearson, 2005.

[Uwano]         Uwano, H., Nakamura, M., Monden, A., and Matsumoto, K. "Analyzing Individual Performance of Source Code Review Using Reviewer's Eye Movement," *Proceedings of the 2006 Symposium on Eye Tracking Research & Applications*, San Diego, March 27-29, 2006.

# Index

**SYMBOLS**

-- decrement operator 21
- subtraction/unary-minus operator 21
! logical-negation operator 21
!= not-equal-to operator 21, 39
# preprocessor token 23
% modulo operator 21
& address/bitwise-and operator 21, 35
&& logical-and operator 11, 21
* indirection/multiplication operator 21
+ addition/unary-plus operator 5, 21
++ increment operator 21
. component selection operator 21
, comma operator 21, 51
; statement terminator 22
/ division operator 21
//, /*, and */ comment delimiters 17
[ ] subscripting operator 21
^ bitwise-xor operator 21, 35
{ } braces 1, 10, 54
( ) parentheses 11, 21, 44
| bitwise-or operator 21, 35
|| logical-or operator 11, 21
< less-than operator 21
<< left-shift operator 21, 35
<= less-or-equal operator 21
=, +=, -=, *=, /=, %=, &=, |=, ^=, ~=, and != assignment operators 21
== equal-to operator 21
-> component-selection operator 21
> greater-than operator 21
>= greater-or-equal operator 21
>> right-shift operator 21, 35
?: ternary operator 21
~ bitwise-negation operator 21, 35

**A**

abbreviations 12, 57-58
**abort()** function 55
acronyms 12, 57-58
algorithms 18
alignment 23, 25, 27
anonymous declarations 33
architecture 1, 2
array subscripts ([ ]) 21
arrays 48, 50, 54
assembly language 8
**assert()** function 17, 46
assignment expressions 52, 54
assignment operators 21, 23
assumptions 18, 19
asynchronous 45, 47, 49
**auto** storage class specifier 14

## B

binary data  35
binary operators  21
bit-fields  35, 37-38
bit ordering  37-38
bitwise operators  35
blank lines  18, 23, 24
blocks of code  10, 23, 24
**bool** type  39
Booleans  8, 39, 49
braces (**{}**)  1, 10, 54
**break** statements  25, 53
bus  37

## C

C run-time  50
C Standard Library  29, 40, 48, 55
C++  7, 5, 8, 17, 29, 48
C++-style comments  17, 18
C90  3, 34, 39
C99  3, 8, 34, 35, 36, 39, 44, 48, 50
call-by-reference  15
call stack  46
carriage return character  28
**case** labels  25, 53
casts  13, 39
**char** type  34, 51
code beautifiers  22, 26
code differencing  6, 9
code reviews  2, 5
comma operator  21, 51
commented-out code  17
comments  3, 6, 8, 17- 20, 24, 31, 32, 42, 54
communication protocols  31
comparisons  35, 56
compiler optimizations  16
compile-time checks  34, 38
compound statements  10
conditional compilation  17
**const** type qualifier  15-16
constants  30, 31, 35, 36, 54, 56
**continue** statements  14
control flow  14
coupling  16, 30

## D

data types  30, 31, 33-39
debug output  17
**default** labels  25, 52-53
defect tracking  2
**#define** directive  8, 15, 30, 44
delay loops  15, 19
design-by-contract  18
design reviews  2
deviations  6
device drivers  8, 31
**do...while** statements  10, 54
double precision  36
**double** type  36
Doxygen tool  18, 20

## E

**else** statements  10, 24, 42, 52
empty statements  10
end-of-line comments  17, 18
end of file  24
**#endif** directive  17, 30
**enum** keyword  33
enumerations  33
equal-to operator (**==**)  3, 56

equivalence tests  36, 56
exceptional circumstances  1, 14
`exit()` function  55
`extern` storage class specifier  30

## F

`false` constant  39, 40, 48
file paths, absolute  31
fixed-point math  36
fixed-width integer types  3, 34, 38
`float32_t` type  36
`float64_t` type  36
`float128_t` type  36
floating point  36
flow charts  18
`for` statements  10, 21, 22, 54
form feed character  28, 42
function prototypes  31, 47
functions  3, 15, 16, 20, 30, 40, 42-43, 45, 46
function-like macros  44

## G

glitches  16
global scope  30
global variables  15-16, 30, 47, 48-49, 50
GNU Indent tool  22
`goto` statements  4, 14, 55

## H

handles for objects  49
hardware failures  1
header file templates  32, 59
header files  29, 30, 31, 32, 42

## I

`#if` directive  17, 23
`if` statements  10, 21, 24, 52
`#ifdef` directive  23
`#ifndef` directive  17, 30
implementation-defined behaviors  3, 35, 38
`#include` directive  30, 31
include files  31
indentation  6, 10, 18, 25-26, 27, 53
infinite loops  45
`INFINITY` constant  36
`inline` keyword  40, 44, 48
inline functions  8, 44
instruction pointer  55
`int` type  34
`int8_t` type  34
`int16_t` type  34, 35
`int32_t` type  3, 34
`int64_t` type  34
interrupts  15, 46-47
interrupt service routines  15, 46-47
`isfinite()` macro  36
ISO C  3, 8, 13, 35, 38

## J

jumps  14, 55

## K

K&R C  48

## L

legacy code  5, 6
libraries  6, 36

`limits.h` header file  36
line feed character  28
line widths  9, 25
line wraps  26
local variables  8, 50
`long` type  34
`long long` type  34
`longjmp()` function  55
loop counters  15, 19, 48, 54
loops  24, 45, 54

## M

macros, preprocessor  30, 31, 40, 44
magic numbers  54
`main()` function  29, 45
`malloc()` function  52
memory-mapped I/O  15
MISRA  4, 5, 35
modules  3, 6, 15, 18, 20, 29-32, 40, 55

## N

naming conventions  4, 21, 29, 33, 40, 48-49
`NAN` constant  36
`NDEBUG` constant  17
nested comments  17
nested if blocks  52
network  37
non-printing characters  28
`NULL` constant  50, 52, 56

## O

operating systems  45, 47
operator precedence  11
optimization, compiler  16, 19

## P

padding bytes  37
parameters  15, 20, 21, 42, 44
parentheses  11, 21, 44
peripheral  37
peripheral drivers  31
peripheral registers  15-16, 33, 37, 47, 49
pointers  15, 21, 48, 50, 54
pointer variables  48
pointer-to-pointer variables  48
portability  1, 2, 3, 34, 38, 49
`#pragma` directive  8, 30, 46
precedence rules  11
preprocessor  17, 23, 28, 30, 38, 44
preprocessor guards  30
preprocessor macros  28, 30, 44
private functions  31, 42
procedures  30, 40-47
processes  45
prototypes  30, 31, 47
public data types  33
public functions  31, 40, 42

## R

readability  2, 24, 43, 50, 54
`register` storage class specifier  4, 14
registers  15-16, 33, 37, 47, 49
relational operators  39
reliability  1, 3
requirements  1
`return` statements  13, 21, 42, 43, 44
RTOS  45

# Embedded C Coding Standard

## S

safety guidelines  2
semicolons  22
`setjmp()` function  55
`short` type  18, 34
side effects  44
signed integers  13, 34, 35, 44
`signed` type specifier  13, 34, 35
singleton objects  47, 49
`sizeof` macro  37, 52, 54
source file templates  32, 60
source files  29, 30, 31, 32
stack  46
`static` storage class specifier  15-16, 42, 46
static analysis  2, 5
static assertions  34, 38
`stdbool.h` header file  39
`stdint.h` header file  34
storage, allocation of  30
strings  34
`struct` keyword  15, 23, 33, 37
struct overlays  15
structures  15, 21, 23, 33, 37-38
structured programming  14
`switch` statements  10, 21, 24, 25, 52, 53
system startup  50

## T

tabs  6, 27
tasks  45
ternary operator (`?:`)  21
threads  15, 45
`true` constant  39, 40, 48
`typedef` keyword  33
typedefs  30, 34

## U

`uint8_t` type  34
`uint16_t` type  34
`uint32_t` type  34
`uint64_t` type  34
unary operators  21
unconditional jumps  14, 55
underscores  29, 33, 40, 48
unhandled cases  53
uninitialized variables  50
`union` keyword  23, 33, 37
unions  15, 23, 33, 37-38
unsigned integers  13, 34, 35, 44
`unsigned` type specifier  13, 34, 35

## V

variable declarations  8, 50, 51
variable initialization  50
variables  3, 8, 15, 16, 23, 33, 36, 39, 40, 48-49, 50, 56
version control  2, 6, 12, 18
`volatile` type qualifier  15-16

## W

`while` statements  10, 21, 54
white space  6, 21-28